The Vagabond

Poems from Punch

R. C. Lehmann

Alpha Editions

This edition published in 2024

ISBN : 9789362094742

Design and Setting By
Alpha Editions
www.alphaedis.com
Email - info@alphaedis.com

Contents

THE VAGABOND

It was deadly cold in Danbury town
  One terrible night in mid November,
  A night that the Danbury folk remember
For the sleety wind that hammered them down,
That chilled their faces and chapped their skin,
  And froze their fingers and bit their feet,
And made them ice to the heart within,
    And spattered and scattered
    And shattered and battered
Their shivering bodies about the street;
And the fact is most of them didn't roam
In the face of the storm, but stayed at home;
While here and there a policeman, stamping
To keep himself warm or sedately tramping
Hither and thither, paced his beat;
Or peered where out of the blizzard's welter
Some wretched being had crept to shelter,
And now, drenched through by the sleet, a muddled
Blur of a man and his rags, lay huddled.

But one there was who didn't care,
Whatever the furious storm might dare,
A wonderful, hook-nosed bright-eyed fellow
In a thin brown cape and a cap of yellow
That perched on his dripping coal-black hair.
A red scarf set off his throat and bound him,
Crossing his breast, and, winding round him,

Flapped at his flank
In a red streak dank;
And his hose were red, with a purple sheen
From his tunic's blue, and his shoes were green.
He was most outlandishly patched together
With ribbons of silk and tags of leather,
And chains of silver and buttons of stone,
And knobs of amber and polished bone,
And a turquoise brooch and a collar of jade,
And a belt and a pouch of rich brocade,
And a gleaming dagger with inlaid blade
And jewelled handle of burnished gold
Rakishly stuck in the red scarf's fold—
A dress, in short, that might suit a wizard
On a calm warm day
In the month of May,
But was hardly fit for an autumn blizzard.

Whence had he come there? Who could say,
As he swung through Danbury town that day,
With a friendly light in his deep-set eyes,
And his free wild gait and his upright bearing,
And his air that nothing could well surprise,
So bright it was and so bold and daring?
He might have troubled the slothful ease
Of the Great Mogul in a warlike fever;
He might have bled for the Maccabees,
Or risen, spurred
By the Prophet's word,

And swooped on the hosts of the unbeliever.

Whatever his birth and his nomenclature,
  Something he seemed to have, some knowledge
  That never was taught at school or college,
But was part of his very being's nature:
  Some ingrained lore that wanderers show
  As over the earth they come and go,
  Though they hardly know what it is they know.

And so with his head upheld he walked,
  And ever the rain drove down;
And now and again to himself he talked
  In the streets of Danbury town.
And now and again he'd stop and troll
A stave of music that seemed to roll
From the inmost depths of his ardent soul;
But the wind took hold of the notes and tossed them
And the few who chanced to be near him lost them.

So, moving on where his fancy listed,
He came to a street that turned and twisted;
And there by a shop-front dimly lighted
He suddenly stopped as though affrighted,
Stopped and stared with his deep gaze centred
On something seen, like a dream's illusion,
Through the streaming glass, mid the queer confusion
Of objects littered on shelf and floor,
And about the counter and by the door—

And then with his lips set tight he entered.

There were rusty daggers and battered breastplates,

And jugs of pewter and carved oak cases,

And china monsters with hideous faces,

And cracked old plates that had once been best plates;

And needle-covers and such old-wivery;

Wonderful chess-men made from ivory;

Cut-glass bottles for wines and brandies,

Sticks once flourished by bucks and dandies;

Deep old glasses they drank enough in,

And golden boxes they took their snuff in;

Rings that flashed on a gallant's knuckles,

Seals and lockets and shining buckles;

Watches sadly in need of menders,

Blackened firedogs and dinted fenders;

Prints and pictures and quaint knick-knackery,

Rare old silver and mere gimcrackery—

Such was the shop, and in its middle

Stood an old man holding a dusty fiddle.

The Vagabond bowed and the old man bowed,

And then the Vagabond spoke aloud.

"Sir," he said, "we are two of a trade,

Each for the other planned and made,

And so we shall come to a fair agreement,

Since I am for you and you're for me meant.

And I, having travelled hither from far, gain

You yourself as my life's best bargain.

But I am one
   Who chaffers for fun,
Who when he perceives such stores of beauty
Outspread conceives it to be his duty
To buy of his visit a slight memento:
Some curious gem of the quattrocento,
Or something equally rare and priceless,
Though its outward fashions perhaps entice less:
A Sultan's slipper, a Bishop's mitre,
Or the helmet owned by a Roundhead fighter,
Or an old buff coat by the years worn thin,
Or—what do you say to the violin?
I'll wager you've many, so you can't miss one,
And I—well, I have a mind for this one,
This which was made, as you must know,
Three hundred years and a year ago
By one who dwelt in Cremona city
For me—but I lost it, more's the pity,
Sixty years back in a wild disorder
That flamed to a fight on the Afghan border;
And, whatever it costs, I am bound to win it,
For I left the half of my full soul in it."

And now as he spoke his eyes began
To shiver the heart of the grey old man;
  And the old man stuttered,
  And "Sir," he muttered,
"The words you speak are the merest riddle,
But-five pounds down, and you own the fiddle!

And I'll choose for your hand, while the pounds you dole out,
A bow with which you may pick that soul out."

So said so done, and our friend again
Was out in the raging wind and rain.
Swift through the twisting street he passed
And came to the Market Square at last,
    And climbed and stood
    On a block of wood
Where a pent-house, leant to a wall, gave shelter
From the brunt of the blizzard's helter-skelter,
And, waving his bow, he cried, "Ahoy!
Now steady your hearts for an hour of joy!"
And so to his cheek and jutting chin
Straight he fitted the violin,
And, rounding his arm in a movement gay,
Touched the strings and began to play.

There hasn't been heard since the world spun round
Such a marvellous blend of thrilling sound.
It streamed, it flamed, it rippled and blazed,
And now it reproached and now it praised,
And the liquid notes of it wove a scheme
That was one-half life and one-half a dream.
And again it scaled in a rush of fire
The glittering peaks of high desire;
Now, foiled and shattered, it rose again
And plucked at the souls and hearts of men;
And still as it rose the sleet came down

In the Market Square of Danbury town.

And now from hundreds of opened doors,
   With quiet paces
   And happy faces,
In ones and twos and threes and fours,
A crowd pressed out to the Market Square
And stood in the storm and listened there.

And, oh, with what a solemn tender strain
The long-drawn music eased their hearts of pain;
And gave them visions of divine content;
   Green fields and happy valleys far away,
And rippling streams and sunshine and the scent
   Of bursting buds and flowers that come in May.
And one spoke in a rapt and gentle voice,
   And bade his friends rejoice,
"For now," he said, "I see, I see once more
My little lass upon a pleasant shore
Standing, as long ago she used to stand,
And beckoning to me with her dimpled hand.
   As in the vanished years,
So I behold her and forget my tears."
And each one had his private joy, his own,
All the old happy things he once had known,
Renewed and from the prisoning past set free,
And mixed with hope and happy things to be.

So for a magic hour the music gushed,

Then faded to a close, and all was hushed,

And the tranced people woke and looked about,

And fell to wondering what had brought them out

On such a night of wind and piercing sleet,

Exposed with hatless heads and thin-shod feet.

Something, they knew, had chased their heavy sadness;

  And for the years to come they still may keep,

    As from a morning sleep,

Some broken gleam of half-remembered gladness.

But the wild fiddler on his feet of flame

Vanished and went the secret way he came.

———————————

SINGING WATER

I heard—'twas on a morning, but when it was and where,
Except that well I heard it, I neither know nor care—
I heard, and, oh, the sunlight was shining in the blue,
A little water singing as little waters do.

At Lechlade and at Buscot, where Summer days are long,
The tiny rills and ripples they tremble into song;
And where the silver Windrush brings down her liquid gems,
There's music in the wavelets she tosses to the Thames.

The eddies have an air too, and brave it is and blithe;
I think I may have heard it that day at Bablockhythe;
And where the Eynsham weir-fall breaks out in rainbow spray
The Evenlode comes singing to join the pretty play.

But where I heard that music I cannot rightly tell;
I only know I heard it, and that I know full well:
I heard a little water, and, oh, the sky was blue,
A little water singing as little waters do.

FOR WILMA

    (AGED FIVE YEARS)

Like winds that with the setting of the sun
   Draw to a quiet murmuring and cease,
So is her little struggle fought and done;
   And the brief fever and the pain
In a last sigh fade out and so release
The lately-breathing dust they may not hurt again.

Now all that Wilma was is made as naught:
  Stilled is the laughter that was erst our pleasure;
The pretty air, the childish grace untaught,
    The innocent wiles,
    And all the sunny smiles,
The cheek that flushed to greet some tiny treasure;
  The mouth demure, the tilted chin held high,
  The gleeful flashes of her glancing eye;
  Her shy bold look of wildness unconfined,
  And the gay impulse of her baby mind
    That none could tame,
That sent her spinning round,
    A spirit of living flame
Dancing in airy rapture o'er the ground—
  All these with that faint sigh are made to be
  Man's breath upon a glass, a mortal memory.

Then from the silent room where late she played,
  Setting a steady course toward the light,
Swifter than thistledown the little shade,
    Reft from the nooks that she had made her own
    And from the love that sheltered, fared alone
Forth through the gloomy spaces of the night,
    Until at last she lit before the gate
    Where all the suppliant shades must stand and wait.

Grim Cerberus, the foiler of the dead,
  Keeping his everlasting vigil there

In deep-mouthed wrath
Athwart the rocky path,
Did at her coming raise his triple head
And lift his bristling hair;
But when he saw our tender little maid
Forlorn, but unafraid,
He blinked his flaming eyes and ceased to frown,
And, fawning on her, smoothed his shaggy crest,
Composed his savage limbs and settled down
With ears laid back and all his care at rest;
And so with kindly aspect beckoned in
The little playmate of his earthly kin.

For often she had tugged old Rollo's mane,
And often Lufra felt the loving check
Of childish arms about her glossy neck—
Lufra and Rollo, who with anxious faces
Now cast about the haunts and hiding-places
To find their friend, but ever cast in vain.

So now, set free from all that can oppress,
And in her own white innocence arrayed,
Made one for ever with all happiness,
Alert she wanders through the starry glade;
Or, where the blissful Shades intone their praise,
She from the lily-covered bowers
Heaping her arms with flowers
Soars and is borne along
The amaranthine the delightful ways,

Gushes the pretty notes and careless trills
  Of her unstudied song,
  And with her music all the joyous valley fills.

Yet, oh ye Powers whose rule is set above
  These fair abodes that ring the firmament,
Spirits of Peace and Happiness and Love,
  And thou, too, mild-eyed Spirit of Content,
Ye will not chide if sometimes in her play
  The child should start and droop her shining head,
    Turning in meek surmise
    Her wistful eyes
Back tow'rd the dimness of our mortal day
  And the loved home from which her soul was sped.
Soon shall our little Wilma learn to be
  Amid the immortal blest
  An unrepining guest,
  Who now, dear heart, is young for your eternity.

CRAGWELL END

I

There's nothing I know of to make you spend
A day of your life at Cragwell End.
It's a village quiet and grey and old,
A little village tucked into a fold
(A sort of valley, not over wide)
Of the hills that flank it on either side.
There's a large grey church with a square stone tower,
And a clock to mark you the passing hour
In a chime that shivers the village calm
With a few odd bits of the 100th psalm.
A red-brick Vicarage stands thereby,
  Breathing comfort and lapped in ease,
With a row of elms thick-trunked and high,
  And a bevy of rooks to caw in these.

'Tis there that the Revd. Salvyn Bent
  (No tie could be neater or whiter than *his* tie)
Maintains the struggle against dissent,
  An Oxford scholar *ex Aede Christi*;
And there in his twenty-minute sermons
He makes mince-meat of the modern Germans,
Defying their *apparatus criticus*
  Like a brave old Vicar,
  A famous sticker
To Genesis, Exodus and Leviticus.
He enjoys himself like a hearty boy

Who finds his life for his needs the aptest;
But the poisoned drop in his cup of joy
  Is the Revd. Joshua Fall, the Baptist,
An earnest man with a tongue that stings—
  The Vicar calls him a child of schism—
Who has dared to utter some dreadful things
  On the vices of sacerdotalism,
    And the ruination
    Of education
  By the Church of England Catechism.

Set in a circle of oak and beech,
  North of the village lies Cragwell Hall;
And stretching far as the eye can reach,
  Over the slopes and beyond the fall
Of the hills so keeping their guard about it
That the north wind never may chill or flout it,
Through forests as dense as that of Arden,
With orchard and park and trim-kept garden,
And farms for pasture and farms for tillage,
The Hall maintains its rule of the village.
    And in the Hall
    Lived the lord of all,
Girt round with all that our hearts desire
Of leisure and wealth, the ancient Squire.
He was the purplest-faced old man
Since ever the Darville race began,
Pompous and purple-faced and proud;
With a portly girth and a voice so loud

You might have heard it a mile away
When he cheered the hounds on a hunting day.
He was hard on dissenters and such encroachers,
He was hard on sinners and hard on poachers;
He talked of his rights as one who knew
That the pick of the earth to him was due:
The right to this and the right to that,
To the humble look and the lifted hat;
The right to scold or evict a peasant,
The right to partridge and hare and pheasant;
The right to encourage discontent
By raising a hard-worked farmer's rent;
The manifest right to ride to hounds
Through his own or anyone else's grounds;
The right to eat of the best by day
And to snore the whole of the night away;
For his motto, as often he explained,
Was "A Darville holds what a Darville gained."
He tried to be just, but that may be
Small merit in one who has most things free;
   And his neighbours averred,
   When they heard the word,
"Old Darville's a just man, is he? Bust his
Gills, we could do without his justice!"

II

The village itself runs, more or less,
On the sinuous line of a letter S,

Twining its little houses through
The twists of the street, as our hamlets do,
For no good reason, so far as I know,
Save that chance has arranged it so.
It's a quaint old ramshackle moss-grown place,
Keeping its staid accustomed pace;
Not moved at all by the rush and flurry,
The mad tempestuous windy hurry
Of the big world tossing in rage and riot,
While the village holds to its old-world quiet.

There's a family grocer, a family baker,
A family butcher and sausage-maker—
A butcher, proud of his craft and willing
To admit that his business in life is killing,
Who parades a heart as soft as his meat's tough—
There's a little shop for the sale of sweet stuff;
There's a maker and mender of boots and shoes
Of the sort that the country people use,
Studded with iron and clamped with steel,
And stout as a ship from toe to heel,
Who announces himself above his entry
As "patronised by the leading gentry."
  There's an inn, "The George";
  There's a blacksmith's forge,
And in the neat little inn's trim garden
The old men, each with his own churchwarden,
Bent and grey, but gossipy fellows,
Sip their innocent pints of beer,

While the anvil-notes ring high and clear
To the rushing bass of the mighty bellows.
And thence they look on a cheerful scene
As the little ones play on the Village Green,
   Skipping about
   With laugh and shout
As if no Darville could ever squire them,
And nothing on earth could tame or tire them.

On the central point of the pleasant Green
The famous stone-walled well is seen
Which has never stinted its ice-cold waters
To generations of Cragwell's daughters.
No matter how long the rain might fail
There was always enough for can and pail—
Enough for them and enough to lend
To the dried-out rivals of Cragwell End.
An army might have been sent to raise
Enough for a thousand washing days
Crowded and crammed together in one day,
One vast soap-sudded and wash-tubbed Monday,
And, however fast they might wind the winch,
The water wouldn't have sunk an inch.
For the legend runs that Crag the Saint,
  At the high noon-tide of a summer's day,
Thirsty, spent with his toil and faint,
  To the site of the well once made his way,
And there he saw a delightful rill
And sat beside it and drank his fill,

Drank of the rill and found it good,

Sitting at ease on a block of wood,

And blessed the place, and thenceforth never

The waters have ceased but they run for ever.

They burnt St. Crag, so the stories say,

And his ashes cast on the winds away,

But the well survives, and the block of wood

Stands—nay, stood where it always stood,

And still was the village's pride and glory

On the day of which I shall tell my story.

Gnarled and knotty and weather-stained,

Battered and cracked, it still remained;

 And thither came,

 Footsore and lame,

On an autumn evening a year ago

The wandering pedlar, Gipsy Joe.

Beside the block he stood and set

His table out on the well-stones wet.

"Who'll buy? Who'll buy?" was the call he cried

As the folk came flocking from every side;

For they knew their Gipsy Joe of old,

His free wild words and his laughter bold:

So high and low all gathered together

By the village well in the autumn weather,

Lured by the gipsy's bargain-chatter

And the reckless lilt of his hare-brained patter.

And there the Revd. Salvyn Bent,

The parish church's ornament,

Stood, as it chanced, in discontent,

And eyed with a look that was almost sinister
The Revd. Joshua Fall, the minister.
And the Squire, it happened, was riding by,
With an angry look in his bloodshot eye,
Growling, as was his wont, and grunting
At the wasted toil of a bad day's hunting;
And he stopped his horse on its homeward way
To hear what the gipsy had to say.

III

Then the pedlar called to the crowd to hear,
And his voice rang loud and his voice rang clear;
And he lifted his head and began to troll
The whimsical words of his rigmarole:—

"Since last I talked to you here I've hurled
My lone way over the wide, wide world.
South and North and West and East
I've fought with man and I've fought with beast;
And I've opened the gates and cleared the bar
That blocks the road to the morning star!

"I've seen King Pharaoh sitting down
On his golden throne in his jewelled crown,
With wizards fanning like anything
To cool the face of the mighty King:
But the King said, 'Wizards are off,' said he;
'Let Joseph the gipsy talk to me.'

"So I sat by the King and began to spout
As the day drew in and the sun went out;
And I sat by the King and spun my tale
Till the light returned and the night grew pale;
And none of the Wizards blinked or stirred
While the King sat drinking it word by word.

"Then he gave me rubies and diamonds old;
He gave me masses of minted gold.
He gave me all that a King can give:
The right to live and to cease to live
Whenever—and that'll be soon, I know—
The days are numbered of Gipsy Joe.

"Then I went and I wandered on and on
Till I came to the kingdom of Prester John;
And there I stood on a crystal stool
And sang the song of 'The First Wise Fool':
Oh, I sang it low and I sang it high
Till John he whimpered and piped his eye.

"Then I drew a tooth from the lively jaw
Of the Prester's ebony Aunt-in-law;
And he bubbled and laughed so long, d'you see,
That his wife looked glum and I had to flee.
So I fled to the place where the Rajahs grow,
A place where they wanted Gipsy Joe.

"*The Rajahs summoned the turbaned hordes*
And gave me sheaves of their inlaid swords;
And the Shah of Persia next I saw,
Who's brother and friend to the Big Bashaw;
And he sent me a rope of turquoise stones
The size of a giant's knuckle-bones.

"*But a little brown Pygmie took my hand*
And rattled me fast to a silver strand,
Where the little brown Pygmie boys and girls
Are cradled and rocked to sleep in pearls.
And the Pygmies flattered me soft and low,
'You are tall; be King of us, Gipsy Joe.'

"*I governed them well for half-a-year,*
But it came to an end, and now I'm here.
Oh, I've opened the gates and cleared the bar,
And I've come, I've come to my friends from far.
I'm old and broken, I'm lame and tired,
But I've come to the friends my soul desired.

"*So it's watches and lockets, and who will buy?*
It's ribbon and lace, and they're not priced high.
If you're out for a ring or a golden chain
You can't look over my tray in vain:
And here is a balsam made of drops
From a tree that's grown by the Æthiops!

"*I've a chip of the tooth of a mastodont*

- 21 -

That's sure to give you the girl you want.
I've a packet of spells to make men sigh
For the lustrous glance of your liquid eye—
But it's much too dark for such wondrous wares,
So back, stand back, while I light my flares!"

Then he lit a match, but his fingers fumbled,
And, striking his foot on a stone, he stumbled;
And the match, released by the sudden shock,
Fell in flame on the old wood-block,
And burnt there very quietly—
But before you could have counted three,
Hardly giving you time to shout,
A red-blue column of fire shot out,
Up and up and ever higher,
A marvellous burst of raging fire,
Lighting the crowd that shrank from its flashes,
   And so decreasing,
   And suddenly ceasing
As the seat of St. Crag was burnt to ashes!

But in the smoke that drifted on the Green
Queer freaks of vision weirdly wrought were seen:
For on that shifting background each one saw
His own reflection and recoiled in awe;
Saw himself there, a bright light shining through him,
Not as he thought himself, but as men knew him.
Before this sudden and revealing sense
Each rag of sham, each tatter of pretence

Withered and vanished, as dissolved in air,
And left the shuddering human creature bare.
But when they turned and looked upon a friend
They saw a sight that all but made amend:
For they beheld him as a radiant spirit
Indued with virtue and surpassing merit,
Not vain or dull or mean or keen for pelf,
But splendid—as he mostly saw himself.
Darville and Fall were drawn to one another,
And both to Bent as to their heart's own brother;
And a strange feeling grew in every breast,
A self-defeating altruistic zest
Which from that moment's flash composed their strife,
Informed their nature and controlled their life.
But when they sought the Gipsy, him they found,
His dark eyes staring, dead upon the ground.

———————————————————————

THE BIRD IN THE ROOM

A robin skimmed into the room,
  And blithe he looked and jolly,
A foe to every sort of gloom,
  And, most, to melancholy.
He cocked his head, he made no sound,
  But gave me stare for stare back,
When, having fluttered round and round,
  He perched upon a chair-back.

I rose; ah, then, it seemed, he knew
  Too late his reckless error:
Away in eager haste he flew,
  And at his tail flew terror.
Now here, now there, from wall to floor,
  For mere escape appealing,
He fled and struck against the door
  Or bumped about the ceiling.

I went and flung each window wide,
  I drew each half-raised blind up;
To coax him out in vain I tried;
  He could not make his mind up.
He flew, he fell, he took a rest,
  And off again he scuffled
With parted beak and panting breast
  And every feather ruffled.

At length I lured him to the sill,

All dazed and undivining;
Beyond was peace o'er vale and hill,
 And all the air was shining.
I stretched my hand and touched him; then
 He made no more resistance,
But left the cramped abode of men
 And flew into the distance.

Is life like that? We make it so;
 We leave the sunny spaces,
And beat about, or high or low,
 In dark and narrow places;
Till, worn with failure, vexed with doubt,
 Our strength at last we rally,
And the bruised spirit flutters out
 To find the happy valley.

KILLED IN ACTION

RUPERT is dead, and RUPERT was my friend;

"Only surviving son of"—so it ran—

"Beloved husband" and the rest of it.

But six months back I saw him full of life,

Ardent for fighting; now he lies at ease

In some obscure but splendid field of France,

His strivings over and his conflicts done.

He was a fellow of most joyous moods

And quaint contrivings, ever on the point

Of shaking fame and fortune by the hand

But always baulked of meeting them at last.

He could not brook—and always so declared—

The weak pomposities of little men,

Scorned all the tin-gods of our petty world,

And plunged headlong into imprudences,

And smashed conventions with a reckless zeal,

Holding his luck and not himself to blame

For aught that might betide when reckoning came.

But he was true as steel and staunch as oak.

And if he pledged his word he bore it out

Unswerving to the finish, and he gave

Whate'er he had of strength to help a friend.

When the great summons came he rushed to arms,

Counting no cost and all intent to serve

His country and to prove himself a man.

Yet he could laugh at all his ardour too

And find some fun in glory, as a child

Laughs at a bauble but will guard it well.
Now he is fall'n, and on his shining brow
Glory has set her everlasting seal.

I like to think how cheerily he talked
Amid the ceaseless tumult of the guns,
How, when the word was given, he stood erect,
Sprang from the trench and, shouting to his men,
Led them forthright to where the sullen foe
Waited their coming; and his brain took fire,
And all was exultation and a high
Heroic ardour and a pulse of joy.
"Forward!" his cry rang out, and all his men
Thundered behind him with their eyes ablaze,
"Forward for England! Clear the beggars out!
Remember—" and death found him, and he fell
Fronting the Germans, and the rush swept on.

Thrice blesséd fate! We linger here and droop
Beneath the heavy burden of our years,
And may not, though we envy, give our lives
For England and for honour and for right;
But still must wear our weary hours away,
While he, that happy fighter, in one leap,
From imperfection to perfection borne,
Breaks through the bonds that bound him to the earth.
Now of his failures is a triumph made;
His very faults are into virtues turned;
And, reft for ever from the haunts of men,

He wears immortal honour and is joined

With those who fought for England and are dead.

EPITAPH

FOR AN ENGLISH SOLDIER AND AN INDIAN SOLDIER
BURIED TOGETHER IN FRANCE

When the fierce bugle thrilled alarm,
  From lands apart these fighters came.
An equal courage nerved each arm,
  And stirred each generous heart to flame.

Now, greatly dead, they lie below;
  Their creed or language no man heeds,
Since for their colour they can show
  The blood-red blazon of their deeds!

TO FLIGHT-LIEUTENANT ROBINSON, V.C.

You with the hawk's eyes and the nerves of steel,
How was it with you when the hurried word
Roused you and sent you swiftly forth to deal
A blow for justice? Sure your pulses stirred,
And all your being leapt to meet the call
Which bade you strike nor spare
Where poised in air
Murder and ravening flame were hid intent to fall.

Alone upon your fearful task you flew,
Where in the vault of heaven the high stars swing,
Alone and upward, lost to mortal view,
Winding about the assassin craft a ring
Of fateful motion, till at last you sped
Through the far tracts of gloom
The bolt of doom,
Shattering the dastard foe to earth with all his dead.

For this we thank you, and we bid you know
That henceforth in the air, by day or night,
A myriad hopes of ours, where'er you go,
Rise as companions of your soaring flight;
And well we know that when there comes the need
A host of men like you,
As staunch, as true,
Will rush to prove the daring of the island breed.

PAGAN FANCIES

Blow, Father Triton, blow your wreathéd horn
  Cheerly, as is your wont, and let the blast
Circle our island on the breezes borne;
  Blow, while the shining hours go swiftly past.
Rise, Proteus, from the cool depths rise, and be
A friend to them that breast your ancient sea.

I shall be there to greet you, for I tire
  Of the dull meadows and the crawling stream.
Now with a heart uplifted and a-fire
  I come to greet you and to catch the gleam
Of jocund Nereids tossing in the air
The sportive tresses of their amber hair.

High on a swelling upland I shall stand
  Stung by the buffets of the wind-borne spray;
Or join the troops that sport upon the sand,
  With shouts and laughter wearing out the day;
Or pace apart and listen to the roar
Of the great waves that beat the crumbling shore.

Then, when the children all are lapped in sleep
  The pretty Nymphlets of the sea shall rise,
And we shall know them as they flit and creep
  And peep and glance and murmur lullabies;
While the pale moon comes up beyond the hill,
And Proteus rests and Triton's horn is still.

ROBIN, THE SEA-BOY

Ho, ruddy-cheeked boys and curly maids,

Who deftly ply your pails and spades,

All you who sturdily take your stand

On your pebble-buttressed forts of sand,

  And thence defy

  With a fearless eye

And a burst of rollicking high-pitched laughter

The stealthy trickling waves that lap you

And the crested breakers that tumble after

To souse and batter you, sting and sap you—

All you roll-about rackety little folk,

Down-again, up-again, not-a-bit brittle folk,

  Attend, attend,

  And let each girl and boy

  Join in a loud "Ahoy!"

For, lo, he comes, your tricksy little friend,

From the clear caverns of his crystal home

Beyond the tossing ridges of the foam:

Planner of sandy romps and wet delights,

Robin the Sea-boy, prince of ocean-sprites,

Is come, is come to lead you in your play

And fill your hearts with mirth and jocund sport to-day!

What! Can't you see him? There he stands

On a sheer rock and lifts his hands,

A little lad not three feet high,

With dancing mischief in his eye.

His body gleams against the light,

A clear-cut shape of dazzling white
Set off and topped by golden hair
That streams and tosses in the air.
A moment poised, he dares the leap
And cuts the wind and cleaves the deep.
Down through the emerald vaults self-hurled
That roof the sea-god's awful world.
Another moment sees him rise
And beat the salt spray from his eyes.
He breasts the waves, he spurns their blows;
Then, like a rocket, up he goes,
Up, up to where the gusty wind
With all its wrath is left behind;
Still up he soars and high and high
A speck of light that dots the sky.
Then watch him as he slowly droops
Where the great sea-birds wheel their troops.
Three broad-winged gulls, himself their lord,
He hitches to a silken cord,
Bits them and bridles them with skill
And bids them draw him where he will.
Above the tumult of the shores
He floats, he stoops, he darts, he soars;
From near and far he calls the rest
And waves them forward for a quest;
Then straight, without a check, he speeds
Across the azure tracts and leads
With apt reproof and cheering words
As on a chase his cry of birds.

And when he has finished his airy fun
And all his flights and his swoops are done
He will drop to the shore and lend a hand
In building a castle of weed and sand.
He will cover with flints its frowning face
To keep the tide in its proper place,
And the waves shall employ their utmost damp art
In vain to abolish your moated rampart.
And nobody's nurse shall make a fuss,
As is far too often the case with us;
Instead of the usual how-de-do
She will give us praise when we get wet through;
In fact she will smile and think it better
When we get as wet as we like and wetter.
As for eating too much, you can safely risk it
With chocolate, lollipop, cake, and biscuit,
And your mother will revel with high delight
In the state of her own one's appetite.
Great shells there shall be of a rainbow hue
To be found and gathered by me and you;
Wonderful nets for the joy of making 'em,
And scores of shrimps for the trouble of taking 'em;
In fact it isn't half bad—now is it?—
When Robin the Sea-boy pays his visit.
And perhaps he will tire of his shape and habit
And change and turn to a frisky rabbit,
A plump young gadabout cheerful fellow
With a twitching nose and a coat of yellow,

And never the smallest trace of fear
From his flashing scut to his flattened ear.

But, lo, there's a hint of coming rain,
So, presto, Robin is back again.
He lifts his head and he cocks his eye
And waves his hand and prepares to fly—
"Good-bye, Robin, good-bye, good-bye!"

THE BIRTHDAY

Sweetheart, where all the dancing joys compete
Take now your choice; the world is at your feet,
All turned into a gay and shining pleasance,
And every face has smiles to greet your presence.
  Treading on air,
  Yourself you look more fair;
And the dear Birthday-elves unseen conspire
To flush your cheeks and set your eyes on fire.

Mayhap they whisper what a birthday means
That sets you spinning through your pretty teens.
A slim-grown shape adorned with golden shimmers
Of tossing hair that streams and waves and glimmers,
  Lo, how you run
  In mere excess of fun,
Or change to silence as you stand and hear
Some kind old tale that moves you to a tear.

And, since this is your own bright day, my dear,
Of all the days that gem the sparkling year,
See, we have picked as well as we were able
And set your gifts upon your own small table:
  A knife from John,
  Who straightway thereupon,
Lest you should cut your friendship for the boy,
Receives a halfpenny and departs with joy.

The burnished inkstand was your mother's choice;

For six new handkerchiefs I gave my voice,

Having in view your tender little nose's

Soft comfort; and the agate pen is Rosie's;

  The torch is Peg's,

  Guide for your errant legs

When ways are dark, and, last, behold with these

A pencil from your faithful Pekinese!

And now the mysteries are all revealed

That were so long, so ardently concealed—

All save the cake which still is in the making,

Not yet smooth-iced and unprepared for taking

  The thirteen flames

  That start the noisy games

Of tea-time, when my happy little maid

Thrones it triumphant, teened and unafraid.

So through the changing years may all delight

Live in your face and make your being bright.

May the good sprites and busy fays befriend you,

And cheerful thoughts and innocent defend you;

  And, far away

  From this most joyous day,

When in the chambers of your mind you see

Those who have loved you, then remember me.

THE DANCE

When good-nights have been prattled, and prayers have been said,

And the last little sunbeam is tucked up in bed,

Then, skirting the trees on a carpet of snow,

The elves and the fairies come out in a row.

  With a preening of wings

  They are forming in rings;

Pirouetting and setting they cross and advance

In a ripple of laughter, and pair for a dance.

And it's oh for the boom of the fairy bassoon,

And the oboes and horns as they strike up a tune,

And the twang of the harps and the sigh of the lutes,

And the clash of the cymbals, the purl of the flutes;

  And the fiddles sail in

  To the musical din,

While the chief all on fire, with a flame for a hand,

Rattles on the gay measure and stirs up his band.

With a pointing of toes and a lifting of wrists

They are off through the whirls and the twirls and the twists;

Thread the mazes of marvellous figures, and chime

With a bow to a curtsey, and always keep time:

  All the gallant and girls

  In their diamonds and pearls,

And their gauze and their sparkles, designed for a dance

By the leaders of fairy-land fashion in France.

But the old lady fairies sit out by the trees,

And the old beaux attend them as pert as you please.

They quiz the young dancers and scorn their display,

And deny any grace to the dance of to-day;

  "In Oberon's reign,"

  So they're heard to complain,

"When we went out at night we could temper our fun

With some manners in dancing, but now there are none."

But at last, though the music goes gallantly on,

And the dancers are none of them weary or gone,

When the gauze is in rags and the hair is awry,

Comes a light in the East and a sudden cock-cry.

  With a scurry of fear

  Then they all disappear,

Leaving never a trace of their gay little selves

Or the winter-night dance of the fairies and elves.

PANSIES

Tufted and bunched and ranged with careless art
Here, where the paving-stones are set apart,
Alert and gay and innocent of guile,
The little pansies nod their heads and smile.

With what a whispering and a lulling sound
They watch the children sport about the ground,
Longing, it seems, to join the pretty play
That laughs and runs the light-winged hours away.

And other children long ago there were
Who shone and played and made the garden fair,
To whom the pansies in their robes of white
And gold and purple gave a welcome bright.

Gone are those voices, but the others came.
Joyous and free, whose spirit was the same;
And other pansies, robed as those of old,
Peeped up and smiled in purple, white and gold.

For pansies are, I think, the little gleams
Of children's visions from a world of dreams,
Jewels of innocence and joy and mirth,
Alight with laughter as they fall to earth.

Below, the ancient guardian, it may hap,
The kindly mother, takes them in her lap,
Decks them with glowing petals and replaces

In the glad air the friendly pansy-faces.

So tread not rashly, children, lest you crush
A part of childhood in a thoughtless rush.
Would you not treat them gently if you knew
Pansies are little bits of children too?

THE DRAGON OF WINTER HILL

I

This is the tale the old men tell, the tale that was told to me,
   Of the blue-green dragon,
   The dreadful dragon,
   The dragon who flew so free,
   The last of his horrible scaly race
   Who settled and made his nesting place
   Some hundreds of thousands of years ago.
   One day, as the light was falling low
   And the turbulent wind was still,
   In a stony hollow,
   Where none dared follow,
Beyond the ridge on the gorse-clad summit, the summit of Winter Hill!

The news went round in the camp that night;
  it was Dickon who brought it first
   How the wonderful dragon,
   The fiery dragon,
  On his terrified eyes had burst.

"I was out," he said, "for a fat young buck,
But never a touch I had of luck;
And still I wandered and wandered on
Till all the best of the day was gone;
When, suddenly, lo, in a flash of flame
Full over the ridge a green head came,

A green head flapped with a snarling lip,
And a long tongue set with an arrow's tip.
I own I didn't stand long at bay,
But I cast my arrows and bow away,
And I cast my coat, and I changed my plan,
And forgot the buck, and away I ran—
  And, oh, but my heart was chill:
    For still as I ran I heard the bellow
    Of the terrible slaughtering fierce-eyed fellow
Who has made his lair on the gorse-clad summit,
    the summit of Winter Hill."

Then the women talked, as the women will, and the men-folk they talked
too
  Of the raging dragon,
  The hungry dragon,
The dragon of green and blue.
And the Bards with their long beards flowing down,
They sat apart and were seen to frown.

But at last the Chief Bard up and spoke,
"Now I swear by beech and I swear by oak,
By the grass and the streams I swear," said he,
"This dragon of Dickon's puzzles me.
For the record stands, as well ye know,
How a hundred years and a year ago
We dealt the dragons a smashing blow
By issuing from our magic tree
A carefully-framed complete decree,
Which ordered dragons to cease to be.

Still, since our Dickon is passing sure

That he saw a regular Simon pure.

Some dragon's egg, as it seems, contrived

To elude our curses, and so survived

On an inaccessible rocky shelf,

Where at last it managed to hatch itself.

Whatever the cause, the result is plain:

We're in for a dragon-fuss again.

We haven't the time, and, what is worse,

We haven't the means to frame a curse.

So what is there left for us to say

Save this, that our men at break of day

  Must gather and go to kill

    The monstrous savage

    Whose fire-blasts ravage

The flocks and herds on the gorse-clad summit,

    the summit of Winter Hill?"

II

So the men, when they heard the Chief Bard utter the order that bade them

    try

  For the awful dragon,

  The dauntless dragon,

They all of them shouted "Aye!"

For everyone felt assured that he,

Whatever the fate of the rest might be,

However few of them might survive,

Was certainly safe to stay alive,

And was probably bound to deal the blow

That would shatter the beast and lay him low,

And end the days of their dragon-foe.

And all the women-folk egged them on:

It was "Up with your heart, and at him, John!"

Or "Gurth, you'll bring me his ugly head,"

Or "Lance, my man, when you've struck him dead,

When he hasn't a wag in his fearful tail,

Carve off and bring me a blue-green scale."

Then they set to work at their swords and spears—

Such a polishing hadn't been seen for years.

They made the tips of their arrows sharp,

Re-strung and burnished the Chief Bard's harp,

Dragged out the traditional dragon-bag,

Sewed up the rents in the tribal flag;

And all in the midst of the talk and racket

Each wife was making her man a packet—

A hunch of bread and a wedge of cheese

And a nubble of beef, and, to moisten these,

A flask of her home-brewed, not too thin,

As a driving force for his javelin

  When the moment arrived to spill

    The blood of the terror

    Hatched out in error

Who had perched his length on the gorse-clad summit,

    the summit of Winter Hill.

The night had taken her feast of stars, and the sun shot up in flame,

When "Now for the dragon!

  Who hunts the dragon?"

The call from the watchers came;

And, shaking the mists of sleep away,

The men stepped into the light of day,

Twice two hundred in loose array;

With a good round dozen of bards to lead them

And their wives all waving their hands to speed them,

While the Chief Bard, fixed in his chair of state,

With his harp and his wreath looked most sedate.

It wasn't his place to fight or tramp;

When the warriors went he stayed in camp;

But still from his chair he harped them on

Till the very last of the host had gone,

Then he yawned and solemnly shook his head

And, leaving his seat, returned to bed,

  To sleep, as a good man will

    Who, braving malice and tittle-tattle,

    Has checked his natural lust for battle,

And sent the rest to the gorse-clad summit,

    the summit of Winter Hill.

III

Marching at ease in the cheerful air, on duty and daring bent,

  In quest of the dragon,

  The fateful dragon,

The fierce four hundred went:

Over the hills and through the plain,

And up the slopes of the hills again.

The sleek rooks, washed in the morning's dew,

Rose at their coming and flapped and flew

In a black procession athwart the blue;

And the plovers circled about on high

With many a querulous piping cry.

And the cropping ewes and the old bell-wether

Looked up in terror and pushed together;

And still with a grim unbroken pace

The men moved on to their battle-place.

Softly, silently, all tip-toeing,

With their lips drawn tight and their eyes all glowing,

With gleaming teeth and straining ears

And the sunshine laughing on swords and spears,

Softly, silently on they go

To the hidden lair of the fearful foe.

They have neared the stream, they have crossed the bridge,

And they stop in sight of the rugged ridge,

And it's "Flankers back!" and "Skirmishers in!"

And the summit is theirs to lose or win—

To win with honour or lose with shame;

And so to the place itself they came,

   And gazed with an awful thrill

    At the ridge of omen,

    Beset by foemen,

At the arduous summit, the gorse-clad summit,

   the summit of Winter Hill.

But where was the dragon, the scale-clad dragon,

 the dragon that Dickon saw,

 The genuine dragon,

 The pitiless dragon,

The dragon that knew no law?

Lo, just as the word to charge rang out,

And before they could give their battle shout,

 On a stony ledge

 Of the ridge's edge,

With its lips curled back and its teeth laid bare,

And a hiss that ripped the morning air,

 With its backbone arched

 And its tail well starched,

With bristling hair and flattened ears,

What shape of courage and wrath appears?

A cat, a tortoiseshell mother-cat!

And a very diminutive cat at that!

And below her, nesting upon the ground,

A litter of tiny kits they found:

Tortoiseshell kittens, one, two, three,

Lying as snug as snug could be.

And they took the kittens with shouts of laughter

And turned for home, and the cat came after.

And when in the camp they told their tale,

The women—but stop! I draw a veil.

The cat had tent-life forced upon her

And was kept in comfort and fed with honour;

 But Dickon has heard his fill

 Of the furious dragon

They tried to bag on

The dragonless summit, the gorse-clad summit,

the summit of Winter Hill!

FLUFFY, A CAT

So now your tale of years is done,
Old Fluff, my friend, and you have won,
Beyond our land of mist and rain,
Your way to the Elysian plain,
Where through the shining hours of heat
A cat may bask and lap and eat;
Where goldfish glitter in the streams,
And mice refresh your waking dreams,
And all, in fact, is planned—and that's
Its great delight—to please the cats.

Yet sometimes, too, your placid mind
Will turn to those you've left behind,
And most to one who sheds her tears,
The mistress of your later years,
Who sheds her tears to summon back
Her faithful cat, the white-and-black.

Fluffy, full well you understood
The frequent joys of motherhood—
To lick, from pointed tail to nape,
The mewing litter into shape;
To show, with pride that condescends,
Your offspring to your human friends,
And all our sympathy to win
For every kit tucked snugly in.

In your familiar garden ground
We've raised a tributary mound,
And passing by it we recite
Your merits and your praise aright.

"Here lies," we say, "from care released
A faithful, furry, friendly beast.
Responsive to the lightest word,
About these walks her purr was heard.
Love she received, for much she earned,
And much in kindness she returned.
Wherefore her comrades go not by
Her little grave without a sigh."

THE LEAN-TO-SHED

(COMMUNICATED BY AN EIGHT-YEAR-OLD)

I've a palace set in a garden fair,

And, oh, but the flowers are rich and rare,

  Always growing

  And always blowing

Winter or summer—it doesn't matter—

For there's never a wind that dares to scatter

The wonderful petals that scent the air

About the walls of my palace there.

And the palace itself is very old,

And it's built of ivory splashed with gold.

It has silver ceilings and jasper floors

And stairs of marble and crystal doors;

And whenever I go there, early or late,

The two tame dragons who guard the gate

And refuse to open the frowning portals

To sisters, brothers and other mortals,

  Get up with a grin

  And let me in.

And I tickle their ears and pull their tails

And pat their heads and polish their scales;

And they never attempt to flame or fly,

Being quelled by me and my human eye.

Then I pour them drink out of golden flagons,

Drink for my two tame trusty dragons...

  But John,

  Who's a terrible fellow for chattering on,

John declares
They are Teddy-bears;
And the palace itself, he has often said,
Is only the gardener's lean-to shed.

In the vaulted hall where we have the dances
There are suits of armour and swords and lances,
Plenty of steel-wrought who's-afraiders,
All of them used by real crusaders;
Corslets, helmets and shields and things
Fit to be worn by warrior-kings,
Glittering rows of them—
Think of the blows of them,
Lopping,
Chopping,
Smashing
And slashing
The Paynim armies at Ascalon...
But, bother the boy, here comes our John
Munching a piece of currant cake,
Who says the lance is a broken rake,
And the sword with its keen Toledo blade
Is a hoe, and the dinted shield a spade,
Bent and useless and rusty-red,
In the gardener's silly old lean-to shed.

And sometimes, too, when the night comes soon
With a great magnificent tea-time moon.
Through the nursery-window I peep and see

My palace lit for a revelry;

And I think I shall try to go there instead

Of going to sleep in my dull small bed.

 But who are these

 In the shade of the trees

 That creep so slow

 In a stealthy row?

They are Indian braves, a terrible band,

Each with a tomahawk in his hand,

And each has a knife *without a sheath*

Fiercely stuck in his gleaming teeth.

Are the dragons awake? Are the dragons sleepers?

Will they meet and scatter these crafty creepers?

What ho! ... But John, who has sorely tried me,

Trots up and flattens his nose beside me;

Against the window he flattens it

 And says he can see

 As well as me,

But never an Indian—not a bit;

Not even the top of a feathered head,

But only a wall and the lean-to shed.

THE CONTRACT

"Come, Peggy, put your toys away; you needn't shake your head,
Your bear's been working overtime; he's panting for his bed.
He's turned a thousand somersaults, and now his head must ache;
It's cruelty to animals to keep the bear awake."

At this she stamped in mutiny, and then she urged her plea,
Her wonted plea, "A little time, a minute more, for me."
"Be off, you little rogue of rogues," I sternly made reply;
"It's wicked to be sitting up with sand in either eye.

"To bed, to bed, you sleepy head; and then, and then—who knows?—
Some day you'll be a grown-up girl, and lovely as a rose.
And some day some one else will come, a gallant youth and gay,
To harry me and marry you and carry you away."

At this the storm broke out afresh:—"You know I hate the boys;
They're only good at taking things, and breaking things, and noise.
So, Daddy, please remember this, because—I—want—you—to:—
I'll never marry any boy; I'll only marry *you*."

"Agreed," I cried—the imp, of course, had won the bout of wits;
Had gained her point and got her time and beaten me to fits—
"Agreed, agreed,"—she danced for joy—"we'll leave no room for doubt,
But bind ourselves with pen and ink, and write the contract out:-"

This is a contract, firm and clear
Made, as doth from these presents appear,
Between Peggy, being now in her sixth year,

A child of laughter,
  A sort of funny actress,
 Referred to hereinafter
  As the said contractress—
Between the said contractress, that is to say,
And a person with whom she is often good enough to play;
Who happens to have been something of a factor
 In bringing her into the world, who, in short, is her father,
And is hereinafter spoken of as the said contractor.
 Now the said contractress declares she would rather
Marry the said contractor than any other.
At the same time she affirms with the utmost steadiness
  Her perfect readiness
 To take any other fellow on as a brother.
 Still, she means to marry her father, and to be his wife,
 And to live happily with him all the rest of her life.
  This contract is made without consideration,
  And is subject to later ratification.
The said contractress had it read through
 to see that nothing was missed,
And she took her pen, and she held it tight
 in a chubby and cramped-up fist,
And she made her mark with a blotted cross,
 instead of signing her name;
And the said contractor he signed in full,
 and they mean to observe the same.

"Now give me, Peg, that old brown shoe, that battered shoe of yours,
I'll stow the contract in its toe, and, if the shoe endures,

When sixteen years or so are gone, I'll hunt for it myself

And take it gently from its drawer, or get it from its shelf.

"And when, mid clouds of scattered rice, through all the wedding whirl

A laughing fellow hurries out a certain graceless girl,

Unless my hand have lost its strength, unless my eye be dim,

I'll lift the shoe, the contract too, and fling the lot at him."

JOHN

He's a boy,
And that's the long and (chiefly) the short of it,
And the point of it and the wonderful sport of it;
  A two-year-old with a taste for a toy,
  And two chubby fists to clutch it and grasp it,
  And two fat arms to embrace it and clasp it;
  And a short stout couple of sturdy legs
  As hard and as smooth as ostrich eggs;
  And a jolly round head, so fairly round
    You could easily roll it,
    Or take it and bowl it
  With never a bump along the ground.

And, as to his cheeks, they're also fat—
I've seen them in ancient prints like that,
    Where a wind-boy high
    In a cloudy sky
  Is puffing away for all he's worth,
    Uprooting the trees
    With a reckless breeze,
  And strewing them over the patient earth,
  Or raising a storm to wreck the ships
  With the work of his lungs and cheeks and lips.

Take a look at his eyes; I put it to you,
Were ever two eyes more truly blue?
If you went and worried the whole world through
You'd never discover a bluer blue;

I doubt if you'd find a blue so true
In the coats and scarves of a Cambridge crew.

   And his hair
   Is as fair
   As a pretty girl's,

But it's right for a boy with its crisp, short curls
All a-gleam, as he struts about
  With a laugh and a shout,
To summon his sister-slaves to him
For his joyous Majesty's careless whim.

But now, as, after a stand, he budges,
And sets to work and solemnly trudges,
Out from a bush there springs full tilt
His four-legged playmate—and John is spilt.

She's a young dog and a strong dog
And a tall dog and a long dog,
A Danish lady of high degree,
Black coat, kind eye and a stride that's free.

   And out she came
   Like a burst of flame,
    And John,
   As he trudged and strutted
    Sturdily on,
   Was blindly butted,

And, all his dignity spent and gone,

    On a patch of clover

    Was tumbled over,

  His two short legs having failed to score

  In a sudden match against Lufra's four.

  But we picked him up

    And we brushed him down,

  And he rated the pup

    With a dreadful frown;

And then he laughed and he went and hugged her,

Seized her tail in his fist and tugged her,

  And so, with a sister's hand to guide him,

  Continued his march with the dog beside him.

And soon he waggles his way upstairs—

He does it alone, though he finds it steep.

He is stripped and gowned, and he says his prayers,

  And he condescends

  To admit his friends

 To a levée before he goes to sleep.

  He thrones it there

  With a battered bear

And a tattered monkey to form his Court,

And, having come to the end of day,

Conceives that this is the time for play

And every possible kind of sport.

But at last, tucked in for the hundredth time,

He babbles a bit of nursery rhyme,

    And on the bed

   Droops his curly round head,

Gives one long sigh of unalloyed content

Over a day so well, so proudly spent,

Resigned at last to listen and obey,

And so begins to breathe his quiet night away.

———————————————

THE SPARROW

Let others from the feathered brood

Which through the garden seeks its food

Pick out for a commending word

Each one his own peculiar bird;

Hail the plump tit, or fitly sing

The finch's crest and flashing wing;

Exalt the rook's black satin dress-coat,

The thrush's speckled fancy waistcoat;

Or praise the robin, meek, but sly,

For breast and tail and friendly eye—

These have their place within my heart;

The sparrow owns the larger part,

And, for no virtues, rules in it,

My reckless cheerful favourite!

Friend sparrow, let the world contemn

Your ways and make a mock of them,

And dub you, if it has a mind,

Low, quarrelsome, and unrefined;

And let it, if it will, pursue

With harsh abuse the troops of you

Who through the orchard and the field

Their busy bills in mischief wield;

Who strip the tilth and bare the tree,

And make the gardener's face to be

Expressive of the words he could,

But must not, utter, though he would

(For gardeners still, where'er they go,

Whate'er they do, in weal or woe,

Through every chance of life retain
Their ancient Puritanic strain;
Tried by the weather they control
Each day their angry human soul,
And, by the sparrow teased, may tear
Their careworn locks, but never swear).
Let us admit—alas,'tis true—
You are not adequately few;
That half your little life is spent
In furious strife or argument;
Still, though your wickedness must harrow
All feeling souls, I love my sparrow;
Still, though I oft and gravely doubt you,
I really could not do without you.
Your pluck, your wit, your nonchalance,
Your cheerful confidence in chance,
Your darting flight, your bouts of play,
Your chirp, so sociable and gay—
These, and no beauty soft or striking,
Make up your passport to my liking;
And for your faults I'll still defend you,
My little sparrow, and befriend you.

GELERT

Tested and staunch through many a changing year,

Gelert, his master's faithful hound, lies here.

Humble in friendship, but in service proud,

He gave to man whate'er his lot allowed;

And, rich in love, on each well-trusted friend

Spent all his wealth and still had more to spend.

Now, reft beyond the unfriendly Stygian tide,

For these he yearns and has no wish beside.

AVE, CAESAR!

(MAY 20, 1910)

Full in the splendour of this morning hour,
  With tramp of men and roll of muffled drums,
In what a pomp and pageantry of power,
  Borne to his grave, our lord, King EDWARD, comes!

In flashing gold and high magnificence,
  Lo, the proud cavalcade of comrade Kings,
Met here to do the dead KING reverence,
  Its solemn tribute of affection brings.

Heralds and Pursuivants and Men-at-arms,
  Sultan and Paladin and Potentate,
Scarred Captains who have baffled war's alarms
  And Courtiers glittering in their robes of state,

All in their blazoned ranks, with eyes cast down,
  Slow pacing in their sorrow pass along
Where that which bore the sceptre and the crown
  Cleaves at their head the silence of the throng.

And in a space behind the passing bier,
  Looking and longing for his lord in vain,
A little playmate whom the KING held dear,
  Caesar, the terrier, tugs his silver chain!

Hail, Caesar, lonely little Caesar, hail!
Little for you the gathered Kings avail.
Little you reck, as meekly past you go,
Of that solemnity of formal woe.
In the strange silence, lo, you prick your ear
For one loved voice, and that you shall not hear.
So when the monarchs with their bright array
Of gold and steel and stars have passed away,
When, to their wonted use restored again,
All things go duly in their ordered train,
You shall appeal at each excluding door,
Search through the rooms and every haunt explore;
From lawn to lawn, from path to path pursue
The well-loved form that still escapes your view.
At every tree some happy memories rise
To stir your tail and animate your eyes,
And at each turn, with gathering strength endued,
Hope, still frustrated, must be still renewed.
How should you rest from your appointed task
Till chance restore the happiness you ask,
Take from your heart the burden, ease your pain,
And grant you to your master's side again,
Proud and content if but you could beguile
His voice to flatter and his face to smile?

Caesar, the kindly days may bring relief;
Swiftly they pass and dull the edge of grief.

You too, resigned at last, may school your mind
To miss the comrade whom you cannot find,
Never forgetting, but as one who feels
The world has secrets which no skill reveals.
Henceforth, whate'er the ruthless fates may give,
You shall be loved and cherished while you live.
Reft of your master, little dog forlorn,
To one dear mistress you shall now be sworn,
And in her queenly service you shall dwell,
At rest with one who loved your master well.
And she, that gentle lady, shall control
The faithful kingdom of a true dog's soul,
And for the past's dear sake shall still defend
Caesar, the dead KING'S humble little friend.

SOO-TI

A PEKINESE

Soo-Ti, I thank the careful fate

That made you wise and obstinate,

Alert, but with a proper pride,

And gay, but wondrous dignified.

I praise your black and tilted nose;

I praise your heart's deep love that shows

In songs made up of whimpering cries

And in the radiance of your eyes

(And if they bulge—forgive the allusion—

Are eyes the worse for such protrusion?

The smaller eyes are, sure, the blinder,

And size makes every kind eye kinder).

Next with affection's look I note

The glossy levels of your coat,

Where a rich black doth most prevail,

Shading to beaver in your tail,

And lightly fading as it reaches

The tufted things you wear as breeches.

The dweller on the cushion purrs

No less when Soo-Ti barks and stirs.

She blinks and blinks and lets you share

Her bowl of milk, her fav'rite chair.

For you she hides her cruel claw

And taps you with a velvet paw;

And, mastered by your lordly air,

For you is meek and debonair.

Even should you growl her hair stays flat:

Be sure she thinks you half a cat.

But you're a Dog and know your job:

Oft have I seen you hob-a-nob,

And grandly gracious to unbend

With a Great Dane, your humble friend.

As on the lawn with him you roll,

He makes your very being droll.

Yet how you set to work to flout him,

To tease and gnaw and dance about him!

You risk the pressure of his paws,

Plunge all you are within his jaws,

And, swelling to a final rage,

With pin-point teeth the fight engage,

While he submits his silly size

To every insult you devise.

At last, withdrawing from the fuss,

You come and tell your tale to us,

Bearing aloft through every room

Your high tail's undefeated plume,

Till, fed with triumphs, you subside,

And sleep and doff your native pride,

Composing in a wicker fane

Those limbs that terrify the Dane.

So, Soo-Ti, I have tried to praise

Yourself and all your winning ways,

Content if I may guard and please
My little dusky Pekinese.

———————————————————

THE BATH

Hang garlands on the bathroom door;
  Let all the passages be spruce;
For, lo, the victim comes once more,
  And, ah, he struggles like the deuce!

Bring soaps of many scented sorts;
  Let girls in pinafores attend,
With John, their brother, in his shorts,
  To wash their dusky little friend.

Their little friend, the dusky dog,
  Short-legged and very obstinate,
Faced like a much-offended frog,
  And fighting hard against his fate.

No Briton he! From palace-born
  Chinese patricians he descends;
He keeps their high ancestral scorn;
  His spirit breaks, but never bends.

Our water-ways he fain would 'scape;
  He hates the customary bath
That thins his tail and spoils his shape,
  And turns him to a fur-clad lath;

And, seeing that the Pekinese
  Have lustrous eyes that bulge like buds,
He fain would save such eyes as these,

Their owner's pride, from British suds.

Vain are his protests—in he goes.
  His young barbarians crowd around;
They soap his paws, they soap his nose;
  They soap wherever fur is found.

And soon, still laughing, they extract
  His limpness from the darkling tide;
They make the towel's roughness act
  On back and head and dripping side.

They shout and rub and rub and shout—
  He deprecates their odious glee—
Until at last they turn him out,
  A damp gigantic bumble-bee.

Released, he barks and rolls, and speeds
  From lawn to lawn, from path to path,
And in one glorious minute needs
  More soapsuds and another bath.

PETER, A PEKINESE PUPPY

Our Peter, who's famed as an eater of things,

Is a miniature dragon without any wings.

He can gallop or trot, he can amble or jog,

But he flies like a flash when he's after his prog;

And the slaves who adore him, whatever his mood,

  Say that nothing is fleeter

  Than Peter the eater,

Than Peter pursuing his food.

He considers the garden his absolute own:

It's the place where a digger can bury a bone.

Then he tests his pin-teeth on a pansy or rose,

Spreading ruin and petals wherever he goes;

And his mistress declares, when he's nibbled for hours,

  That nothing is sweeter

  Than Peter the eater,

The resolute eater of flowers.

Having finished his dinner he wheedles the cook,

Picks a coal from the scuttle or tackles a book,

Or devotes all his strength to a slipper or mat,

To the gnawing of this and the tearing of that;

Faute de mieux takes a dress; and his mistress asserts

  That there's nothing to beat her

  Like Peter the eater

Attached by his teeth to her skirts.

But at last he has supped, and the moment is come

When, his stretchable turn being tight as a drum,

He is meek and submissive, who once was so proud,

And he creeps to his basket and slumbers aloud.

And his mistress proclaims, as she tucks up his shawl,

That nothing is neater

Than Peter the eater,

Than Peter curled up in a ball,

Asleep and digesting it all.

THE DOGS' WELCOME

Hush! We're not a pack of boys
Always bound to make a noise.
　True, there's one amongst us, but
　He is young;
And, wherever we may take him,
　We can generally shut
Such a youngster up and make him
　Hold his tongue.

Hush! Most cautiously we go
On the tippest tip of toe.
　Are the dogs expecting us
　At the gate?
Two, who usually prize us,
　Will they jump and make a fuss?
Will they really recognise us
　Where they wait?

　Hush! I hear the funny pair
　Softly whimpering—yes, they're there.
Dane and Pekinese, they scratch
　　At the wood,
　At the solid wood between us;
Duke attempts to lift the latch;
　It's a month since they have seen us—
　　Open! Good!

Down, Duke, down! Enough, enough!

Soo-Ti's screaming; seize his scruff.

  Soo-Ti's having fearful fits;

  Duke is tearing us to bits.

One will trip us, one will throw us—

But, the darlings, *don't* they know us!

Then off with a clatter the long dog leapt, and, oh, what a race he ran,

At the hurricane pace of a minute a mile, as only a long dog can.

Into and out of the bushes he pierced like a shooting star;

And now he thundered around us, and now he was whirling far.

And the little dog gazed till he seemed amazed,

    and then he took to it too;

With shrill notes flung from his pert pink tongue

    right after his friend he flew;

And the long legs lashed and the short legs flashed

    and scurried like anything,

While Duke ran round in a circle and Soo-Ti ran in a ring.

And last they hurtled amongst us, and then there were tales to tell,

For all of us seemed to be scattered and torn,

    and all of us shrieked and fell;

And John, who is plump, got an awful bump,

    and Helen, who's tall and thin,

Was shot through a shrub and gained in bruise

    as much as she lost in skin;

And Rosamond's frock was rent in rags, and tattered in strips was Peg's,

And both of them suffered the ninepin fate to the ruin of arms and legs;

And every face was licked by a dog, and battered was every limb,

When Duke ran round in a circle and Soo-Ti ran after him.

ODE TO JOHN BRADBURY

(THE NOTES FOR £1 AND 10S ARE SIGNED BY JOHN
BRADBURY)

When the Red KAISER, swoll'n with impious pride
  And stuffed with texts to serve his instant need,
Took Shame for partner and Disgrace for guide,
  Earned to the full the hateful traitor's meed,
    And bade his hordes advance
Through Belgium's cities towards the fields of France;
And when at last our patient island race,
    By the attempted wrong
    Made fierce and strong,
Flung back the challenge in the braggart's face,
Oh then, while martial music filled the air,
  Clarion and fife and bagpipe and the drum,
Calling to men to muster, march, and dare,
  Oh, then thy day, JOHN BRADBURY, was come.

JOHN BRADBURY, the Muse shall fill my strain
  To sing thy praises; thou hadst spent thy time
Not idly, nor hadst lived thy life in vain,
  Unfitted for the guerdon of my rhyme.
For lo, the Funds went sudden crashing down,
  And men grew pale with monetary fear,
    And in the toppling mart
    The stoutest heart
Melted, and fortunes seemed to disappear;
And some, forgetting their austere renown,

Went mad and sold
Whate'er they could and wildly called for Gold!

"Since through no fault of ours the die was cast
    We shall go forth and fight
    In death's despite
And shall return victorious at the last;
    But how, ah how," they said,
    "Shall we and ours be fed
And clothed and housed from dreary day to day,
If, while our hearths grow cold, we have no coin to pay?"

Then thou, where no gold was and little store
    Of silver, didst appear and wave thy pen,
    And with thy signature
    Make things secure,
Bidding us all pluck up our hearts once more
    And face our foolish fancied fears like men.
"I give you notes," you said, "of different kinds
    To ease your anxious minds:
The one is black and shall be fairly found
Equal in value to a golden pound;
The other—mark its healthy scarlet print—
Is worth a full half-sovereign from the Mint."

Thus didst thou speak—at least I think thou didst—
    And, lo, the murmurs fell
    And all things went right well,
While thy notes fluttered in our happy midst.

Therefore our grateful hearts go forth to thee,
Our British note-provider, brave JOHN BRADBURY!

TEETH-SETTING

(1914)

When the thunder-shaking German hosts are marching over France—
Lo, the glinting of the bayonet and the quiver of the lance!—
When a rowdy rampant KAISER, stout and mad and middle-aged,
Strips his breast of British Orders just to prove that he's enraged;

    When with fire and shot and pillage

    He destroys each town and village;

When the world is black with warfare, then there's one thing you must
do:

Set your teeth like steel, my hearties, and sit tight and see it through.
Oh, it's heavy work is fighting, but our soldiers do it well—

    Lo, the booming of the batteries, the clatter of the shell!—

And it's weary work retiring, but they kept a dauntless front,
All our company of heroes who have borne the dreadful brunt.

    They can meet the foe and beat him,

    They can scatter and defeat him,

For they learnt a steady lesson (and they taught a lesson, too),
Having set their teeth in earnest and sat tight and seen it through.
Then their brothers trooped to join them, taking danger for a bride,
Not in insolence and malice, but in honour and in pride;
Caring nought to be recorded on the muster-roll of fame,
So they struck a blow for Britain and the glory of her name.

    Toil and wounds could but delight them,

    Death itself could not affright them,

Who went out to fight for freedom and the red and white and blue,
While they set their teeth as firm as flint and vowed to see it through.

THE DEATH OF EUCLID

["Euclid, we are told, is at last dead, after two thousand years of an immortality that he never much deserved."—*The Times Literary Supplement.*]

A THRENODY for EUCLID! This is he
  Who with his learning made our youth a waste,
Holding our souls in fee;
  A god whose high-set crystal throne was based
Beyond the reach of tears,
Deeper than time and his relentless years!

Come then, ye Angle-Nymphs, and make lament;
  Ye little Postulates, and all the throng
Of Definitions, with your heads besprent
  In funeral ashes, ye who long
Worshipped the King and followed in his train;
For he is dead and cannot rise again.

Then from the shapes that beat their breasts and wept,
Soft to the light a gentle Problem stepped,
And, lo, her clinging robe she swiftly loosed
And with majestic hands her side produced:

"Sweet Theorem," she said, and called her mate,
  "Sweet Theorem, be with me at this hour.
How oft together in a dear debate
  We two bore witness to our Sovereign's power.
But he is dead and henceforth all our days

Are wrapped in gloom,

And we who never ceased to sing his praise

May weep our lord, but cannot call him from his tomb."

And, as they bowed their heads and to and fro

Wove in a mournful gait their web of woe,

    Two sentinels forth came,

    Their hearts aflame,

And moved behind the pair:

    "Warders we are," they cried,

"Of these two sisters who were once so fair,

    So joyous in their pride."

And now their massy shields they lifted high,

    Embossed with letters three,

And, though a mist of tears bedimmed each eye,

    The sorrowing Nymphs could see

Q., E. and F. on one, and on the other Q. E. D.

But on a sudden, with a hideous noise

Of joy and laughter rushed a rout of boys;

    And all the mourners in affright

    Scattered to left and right.

  Problems and Theorems and Angles too,

  Postulates, Definitions, Circles, Planes,

    A jibbering crew,

    With all their hoary gains

Of knowledge, from their monarch dead

Into the outer darkness shrieking fled.

And now with festal dance and laughter loud

Broke in the boyish and intruding crowd;

    Nor did they fail,

Seeing that all the painful throng was sped,

    To let high mirth prevail,

And raise the song of joy for EUCLID dead.

TO POSTUMOUS IN OCTOBER

When you and I were younger the world was passing fair;
Our days were sped with laughter, our steps were free as air;
Life lightly lured us onward, and ceased not to unroll
In endless shining vistas a playground for the soul.
But now no glory fires us; we linger in the cold,
And both of us are weary, and both are growing old;
Come, Postumus, and face it, and, facing it, confess
Your years are half a hundred, and mine are nothing less.

When you and I were twenty, my Postumus, we kept
In tidy rooms in College, and there we snugly slept.
And still, when I am dreaming, the bells I can recall
That ordered us to chapel or welcomed us to hall.
The towers repeat our voices, the grey and ancient Courts
Are filled with mirth and movement, and echo to our sports;
Then riverward we trudge it, all talking, once again
Down all the long unlovely extent of Jesus Lane.

One figure leads the others; with frank and boyish mien,
Straight back and sturdy shoulders, he lords it o'er the scene;
His grip is firm and manly, his cheeks are smooth and red;
The tangled curls cling tightly about his jolly head.
And when we launch the eight-oar I hear his orders ring;
With dauntless iteration I see his body swing:
The pride of all the river, the mainstay of our crew—
O Postumous, my bold one, can this be truly you?

Nay, Postumus, my comrade, the years have hurried on;

You're not the only Phoenix, I know, whose plumes are gone.

When I recall your splendour, your memory, too, is stirred;

You too can show a moulted, but once refulgent, bird;

And, if I still should press you, you too could hardly fail

To point a hateful moral where I adorned the tale.

'Twere better to be thankful to Heaven that ruled it so,

And gave us for our spending the days of long ago.

A RAMSHACKLE ROOM

When the gusts are at play with the trees on the lawn,
  And the lights are put out in the vault of the night;
When within all is snug, for the curtains are drawn,
  And the fire is aglow and the lamps are alight,
Sometimes, as I muse, from the place where I am
  My thoughts fly away to a room near the Cam.

'Tis a ramshackle room, where a man might complain
  Of a slope in the ceiling, a rise in the floor;
With a view on a court and a glimpse on a lane,
  And no end of cool wind through the chinks of the door;
With a deep-seated chair that I love to recall,
  And some groups of young oarsmen in shorts on the wall.

There's a fat jolly jar of tobacco, some pipes—
  A meerschaum, a briar, a cherry, a clay—
There's a three-handled cup fit for Audit or Swipes
  When the breakfast is done and the plates cleared away.
There's a litter of papers, of books a scratch lot,
  Such as *Plato*, and *Dickens*, and *Liddell and Scott*.

And a crone in a bonnet that's more like a rag
  From a mist of remembrance steps suddenly out;
And her funny old tongue never ceases to wag
  As she tidies the room where she bustles about;
For a man may be strong and a man may be young,
  But he can't put a drag on a Bedmaker's tongue.

And, oh, there's a youngster who sits at his ease

   In the hope, which is vain, that the tongue may run down,

With his feet on the grate and a book on his knees,

   And his cheeks they are smooth and his hair it is brown.

Then I sigh myself back to the place where I am

   From that ramshackle room near the banks of the Cam.

THE LAST STRAW

I sing the sofa! It had stood for years,
  An invitation to benign repose,
A foe to all the fretful brood of fears,
  Bidding the weary eye-lid sink and close.
Massive and deep and broad it was and bland—
In short the noblest sofa in the land.

You, too, my friend, my solid friend, I sing,
  Whom on an afternoon I did behold
Eying—'twas after lunch—the cushioned thing,
  And murmuring gently, "Here are realms of gold,
And I shall visit them," you said, "and be
The sofa's burden till it's time for tea."

"Let those who will go forth," you said, "and dare,
  Beyond the cluster of the little shops,
To strain their limbs and take the eager air,
  Seeking the heights of Hedsor and its copse.
I shall abide and watch the far-off gleams
Of fairy beacons from the world of dreams."

Then forth we fared, and you, no doubt, lay down,
  An easy victim to the sofa's charms,
Forgetting hopes of fame and past renown,
  Lapped in those padded and alluring arms.
"How well," you said, and veiled your heavy eyes,
"It slopes to suit me! This is Paradise."

So we adventured to the topmost hill,
  And, when the sunset shot the sky with red,
Homeward returned and found you taking still
  Deep draughts of peace with pillows 'neath your head.
"His sleep," said one, "has been unduly long."
Another said, "Let's bring and beat the gong."

"Gongs," said a third and gazed with looks intent
  At the full sofa, "are not adequate.
There fits some dread, some heavy, punishment
  For one who sleeps with such a dreadful weight.
Behold with me," he moaned, "a scene accurst.
The springs are broken and the sofa's burst!"

Too true! Too true! Beneath you on the floor
  Lay blent in ruin all the obscure things
That were the sofa's strength, a scattered store
  Of tacks and battens and protruded springs.
Through the rent ticking they had all been spilt,
  Mute proofs and mournful of your weight and guilt.

And you? You slept as sweetly as a child,
  And when you woke you recked not of your shame,
But babbled greetings, stretched yourself and smiled
  From that eviscerated sofa's frame,
Which, flawless erst, was now one mighty flaw
  Through the addition of yourself as straw.

THE OLD GREY MARE

There's a line of rails on an upland green
  With a good take-off and a landing sound,
Six fences grim as were ever seen,
And it's there I would be with fox and hound.
Oh, that was a country free and fair
For the raking stride of my old grey mare!

With her raking stride, and her head borne high,
  And her ears a-prick, and her heart a-flame,
And the steady look of her deep brown eye,
  I warrant the grey mare knew the game:
It was "Up to it, lass," and before I knew
We were up and over, and on we flew.

The rooks from the grass got up, and so,
  With a caw and flap, away they went;
When the grey mare made up her mind to go
  At the tail of the bounds on a breast-high scent,
The best of the startled rooks might fail
To match her flight over post and rail.

While some of the thrusters grew unnerved,
  And looked and longed for an open gate,
And one crashed down and another swerved,
  She went for it always true and straight:
She pounded the lot, for she made it good
With never a touch of splintered wood.

Full many a year has come and gone

Since last she gathered her spring for me,

And lifted me up, and so flew on

Unchecked in a country fair and free.

I've ridden a score since then, but ne'er

Crossed one that could live with the old grey mare.

———————————————————

AT PUTNEY

When eight strong fellows are out to row,
  With a slip of a lad to guide them,
I warrant they'll make the light ship go,
  Though the coach on the launch may chide them,
With his "Six, get on to it! Five, you're late!
Don't hurry the slides, and use your weight!
You're bucketing, Bow; and, as to Four,
The sight of his shoulders makes me sore!"

But Stroke has steadied his fiery men,
  And the lift on the boat gets stronger;
And the Coxswain suddenly shouts for "Ten!
  Reach out to it, longer, longer!"
While the wind and the tide raced hand in hand
The swing of the crew and the pace were grand;
But now that the two meet face to face
It's buffet and slam and a tortoise-pace.

For Hammersmith Bridge has rattled past,
  And, oh, but the storm is humming.
The turbulent white steeds gallop fast;
  They're tossing their crests and coming.
It's a downright rackety, gusty day,
And the backs of the crew are drenched in spray;
But it's "Swing, boys, swing till you're deaf and blind,
And you'll beat and baffle the raging wind."

They have slipped through Barnes; they are round thebend;

And the chests of the eight are tightening.
"Now spend your strength, if you've strength to spend,
  And away with your hands like lightning!
Well rowed!"—and the coach is forced to cheer—
"Now stick to it, all, for the post is near!"
And, lo, they stop at the coxswain's call,
With its message of comfort, "Easy all!"

So here's to the sturdy undismayed
  Eight men who are bound together
By the faith of the slide and the flashing blade
  And the swing and the level feather;
To the deeds they do and the toil they bear;
To the dauntless mind and the will to dare;
And the joyous spirit that makes them one
Till the last fierce stroke of the race is done.

"A LITTLE BIT OF BLUE"

When the waves rise high and higher as they toss about together,
And the March-winds, loosed and angry, cut your chilly heart in two,
Here are eighteen gallant gentlemen who come to face the weather
All for valour and for honour and a little bit of blue!

Chorus.
  Oh get hold of it and shove it!
    It is labour, but you love it;
  Let your stroke be long and mighty; keep your body on the swing;
    While your pulses dance a measure
    Full of pride and full of pleasure.
  And the boat flies free and joyous like a swallow on the wing.

Isis blessed her noble youngsters as they left her; Father Camus
Sped his youths to fame and Putney from his grey and ancient Courts:—
"Keep," they said, "the old traditions, and we know you will not shame us
When you try the stormy tideway in your zephyrs and your shorts.

"For it's toil and tribulation till your roughnesses are polished,
And it's bitterness and sorrow till the work of oars is done;
But it's high delight and triumph when your faults are all abolished,
With yourself and seven brothers firmly welded into one."

So they stood the weary trial and the people poured to greet them,
Filled a cup with praise and welcome—it was theirs to take and quaff;
And they ranged their ships alongside, and the umpire came to meet them,
And they stripped themselves and waited till his pistol sent them off.

With a dash and spurt and rally; with a swing and drive and rattle,

Both the boats went flashing faster as they cleft the swelling stream;

And the old familiar places, scenes of many a sacred battle,

Just were seen for half a moment and went by them in a dream.

But at last the flag has fallen and the splendid fight is finished,

And the victory is blazoned on the record-roll of Fame.

They are spent and worn and broken, but their soul is undiminished;

There are winners now and losers, but their glory is the same!

Chorus.

Oh get hold of it and shove it!

It is labour, but you love it;

Let your stroke be long and mighty; keep your body on the swing;

While your pulses dance a measure

Full of pride and full of pleasure,

And the boat flies free and joyous like a swallow on the wing.

THE LAST COCK-PHEASANT

Splendour, whom lately on your glowing flight
  Athwart the chill and cheerless winter-skies
I marked and welcomed with a futile right,
  And then a futile left, and strained my eyes
To see you so magnificently large,
Sinking to rest beyond the fir-wood's marge—

Not mine, not mine the fault: despise me not
  In that I missed you; for the sun was down,
And the dim light was all against the shot;
  And I had booked a bet of half-a-crown.
My deadly fire is apt to be upset
By many causes—always by a bet.

Or had I overdone it with the sloes,
  Snared by their home-picked brand of ardent gin
Designed to warm a shivering sportsman's toes
  And light a fire his reckless head within?
Or did my silly loader put me off
With aimless chatter in regard to golf?

You too, I think, displayed a lack of nerve;
  You did not quite-now did you?-play the game;
For when you saw me you were seen to swerve,
  Doubtless in order to disturb my aim.
No, no, you must not ask me to forgive
A swerve because you basely planned to live.

At any rate I missed you, and you went,
  The last day's absolutely final bird,
Scathless, and left me very ill content;
  And someone (was it I?) pronounced a word,
A word which rather forcible than nice is,
A little word which does not rhyme with Isis.

Farewell! I may behold you once again
  When next November's gales have stripped the leaf.
Then, while your upward flight you grandly strain,
  May I be there to add you to my sheaf;
And may they praise your tallness, saying "This
Was such a bird as men are proud to miss!"

―――――――――――――――――

IN MEMORIAM

FRANCIS COWLEY BURNAND, 1836-1917

EDITOR OF "PUNCH," 1880-1906

Hail and Farewell, dear Brother of the Pen,
Maker of sunshine for the minds of men,
Lord of bright cheer and master of our hearts—
What plaint is fit when such a friend departs?
Not with mere ceremonial words of woe
Come we to mourn—you would not have it so;
But with our memories stored with joyous fun,
Your constant largesse till your life was done,
With quips, that flashed through frequent twists and bends,
Caught from the common intercourse of friends;
And gay allusions gayer for the zest
Of one who hurt no friend and spared no jest.
What arts were yours that taught you to indite
What all men thought, but only you could write!

That wrung from gloom itself a fleeting smile;
Rippled with laughter but refrained from guile;
Led you to prick some bladder of conceit
Or trip intrusive folly's blundering feet,
While wisdom at your call came down to earth,
Unbent awhile and gave a hand to mirth!

You too had pondered mid your jesting strife
The deeper issues of our mortal life;

Guided to God by faith no doubt could dim,
You fought your fight and left the rest to Him,
Content to set your heart on things above
And rule your days by laughter and by love.

Rest in our memories! You are guarded there
By those who knew you as you lived and were.
There mid our Happy Thoughts you take your stand,
A sun-girt shade, and light that shadow-land.

Milton Keynes UK
Ingram Content Group UK Ltd.
UKHW030742071024
449371UK00006B/623